Philosopurrs

Philosopurrs

by

C.B. Daniels

YUL LLC Publishing

2024

The characters and summaries of philosophies portrayed in this book are fictitious. The philosophers mentioned in this book were not in actuality cats, at least not to my knowledge, and have been portrayed as such because I thought it would be cute and good way to introduce people to different philosophies.

No cats were harmed in the making of this book.

No artists names were used in the prompts for the images and the only styles used in the prompts were "minimalist" and "photo".

ISBN 978-1-942116-12-7

Book Cover by Midjourney

Illustrations by Midjourney

First printing, 2024

Email: cbdaniels@artificial-ideas.com

*To my son whose love of cats, history, and silliness
inspired this book.*

*And to my loving wife who graciously humors me and
my endless rants about AI.*

TABLE OF CONTENTS

Preface vi

Introduction viii

THE PHILOSOPURRS
Roughly in order of birth

Lao Tzu 2	Gottfried Wilhelm Leibniz . . . 32
Confucius 4	Voltaire 34
Socrates 6	David Hume 36
Plato 8	Jean-Jacques Rousseau 38
Zhuangzi 10	Immanuel Kant 40
Aristotle 12	Arthur Schopenhauer 42
Epicurus 14	John Stuart Mill 44
Nāgārjuna 16	Rabindranath Tagore 46
Avicenna 18	Bertrand Russell 48
Maimonides 20	Ludwig Wittgenstein 50
Rumi 22	Jean-Paul Sartre 52
Thomas Aquinas 24	Hannah Arendt 54
René Descartes 26	Simone de Beauvoir 56
John Locke 28	Albert Camus 58
Baruch Spinoza 30	Michel Foucault 60

Author's note 62

PREFACE

Why write a book about philosopher cats?

The amusement I get from cats dressed in human clothes, juxtaposed with serious philosophy, certainly played a part. There's just something about the absurdity of a cat in the clothes of a philosopher that makes me smile.

I also aimed to create something that was both fun and educational in equal measures—a goal that, at least for myself, I believe I have achieved. In the course of writing this book, I learned a lot and gained a new respect for some of the philosophies and philosophers featured within. I can only hope that you will, too.

But the main reason? Simply because I could.

Generative AI tools like GPT-4, Mistral, Claude, and Midjourney made this book feasible and cost-effective for one person to tackle on their own, making things that were impossible before, possible.

I have mixed feelings about these AI tools and the impact they will have on the world. After all, they are in the process of replacing the work I did before. More on that in the author's note. But there's no denying how incredibly powerful they are.

So, I took the opportunity to try them out and create something a little off the beaten path. Something I wouldn't normally attempt.

And so, please, read on and enjoy. I hope you come away with a smile and a bit of wisdom.

C.B. Daniels
Author

INTRODUCTION

Each of the following feline philosopurrs are based on real philosophers that you can research and learn more about. Their advice to you is based on the real philosopher's ideas, but seen through the playful lens of a feline version of themselves.

Each mini lecture will give you a small taste of their philosophy and overall message, hopefully enough whet your appetite for more. The mini lectures are created through a collaboration between me and AI. But the "meowtivational" quotes adorning each passage are quotes from the actual human philosophers, serving as a bridge between our playful reimagining and the actual philosopher.

I aimed to make the philosopher cats period-accurate in both their clothing and backgrounds to match the era each thinker lived in. Where possible, I designed the cats' appearances to resemble the real philosophers based on historical paintings and photographs, though some likenesses worked better than others. In certain cases, I represented philosophers with cat breeds originating from their home countries, but this wasn't always feasible.

I strived to strike a balance between an engaging, amusing tone while still faithfully conveying the essence of each philosophical message to maximize the book's educational value. As you progress through the pages, note how both the fashion styles and the philosophies themselves evolve over time, reflecting the changing eras and realities that shaped each thinker's perspective. These were not merely historical figures, but real people whose lived experiences, much like our own, informed their philosophical worldviews and ideas.

I encourage you to look more into any of the philosophers that catch your attention and to learn more about the actual philosopher and their philosophy. You might just find a new philosophical lens to view the world that really resonates with you.

If you are interested in learning more about any of the philosophers and their philosophy, I encourage you to explore that feline curiosity. Read their original works, read commentaries about their philosophy, get a summary of the philosophy or philosopher from your AI of choice, or have AI role play as the philosopher and have a discussion.

Philosophy is the rational investigation of the truths and principles of being, knowledge, or conduct.

- Claude 3 Sonnet

I ponder the Tao, the Way, as I tread lightly upon this Earth. The Tao is ever elusive, escaping just as one thinks they've caught it, yet it guides all things gently, with a silent paw.

Consider the virtue of water; it flows to the lowest of places. Yet, in its humility lies its strength. Be like water, nurturing without seeking reward, flowing with a gentle purr that soothes the troubled spirit.

Remember that the world is constantly changing, and that adaptability is key to navigating life's challenges. Like a cat adjusting its position to maintain balance, learn to be flexible and resilient in the face of adversity. By embracing change and accepting the impermanence of all things, you will find greater peace and stability.

Embrace the principle of Wu Wei, or effortless action. Like a cat gracefully leaping from one perch to another, learn to move through life with ease and spontaneity. By acting in accordance with the natural flow of the Tao, you will find that your actions become more effective and less forced.

To know others is wise, but to know oneself is to be enlightened. Conquer oneself like mastering the art of balance on the narrowest of ledges. Contentment is a warm spot in the sun; endurance, the patience of a hunter. To keep one's place in the world is to understand the perfect spot to rest, to be remembered is to leave gentle paw prints on the hearts of those you touch.

Understand that the nature of the Tao is inherently paradoxical and beyond comprehension. Like a cat attempting to grasp the elusive red dot of a laser pointer, we can never truly pin down the essence of the Tao. Accept this mystery and embrace the paradoxes that life presents, for it is in the acceptance of uncertainty that we find true wisdom.

In observing the world, notice how softness overcomes the hard, as the gentle padding of paws moves silently over rugged terrain. The world is won by those who let go. When desires are set aside, the essence is clear, like the focused gaze upon a single point.

Mystery upon mystery, the gateway to all wonders, is like the cat who sits in the doorway, existing in two worlds, yet belonging to neither.

"Knowing others is intelligence; knowing yourself is true wisdom.
Mastering others is strength; mastering yourself is true power."

In the realms of family and society, the principles of filial piety and fraternal submission intertwine like intertwined tails in a litter. Harmony within the family serves as the cornerstone for harmony within the state. A well-ordered house, where each knows and performs their role, brings peace and stability, much like a cat finds comfort in the familiar corners of its home.

The cultivation of the self, much like the meticulous grooming of one's fur, is a daily task of utmost importance. It requires patience and persistence, for only through constant refinement can one achieve a state of moral perfection. The art of reflection and learning mirrors the attentive watchfulness of a cat at a window, endlessly curious, forever seeking understanding.

Your concept of humaneness, the act of loving others, finds its parallel in the gentle nudge of a feline companion, seeking connection and offering comfort. This principle, akin to the universal language of a purr, transcends boundaries and fosters a deep, unspoken understanding. Foster this in your life and relationships with others.

Family and friends are of utmost importance. A cat's devotion to its loved ones is a testament to the power of connection and belonging. Nurture these relationships, and you will find solace and support in the company of those who care for you.

Seeking the 'Mean', the balance in all things, is akin to the poised stance of a cat, perfectly centered, agile and ready. In this balance, one finds the path to harmony, avoiding the extremes of too much or too little, much as a cat measures its leap or its rest.

Understand the significance of rituals and traditions. Just as a cat engages in daily grooming and hunting routines, so too should you appreciate the value of established customs and practices. By respecting and participating in these rituals, you will create a sense of order and continuity in your life.

Thus, the journey of life, much like a cat's quiet, observant stroll through its domain, is a pursuit of harmony, balance, and understanding. In the gentle grace of our actions, the quiet dignity of our conduct, and the warm embrace of our relationships, we find the essence of a life well-lived.

"Our greatest glory is not in never falling,
but in rising every time we fall."

SOCRATES
470 - 399 BCE

In this world, brimming with endless curiosity and myriad paths, our task is to navigate with both caution and boldness, ever questioning, ever pondering the nature of the good life.

What is virtue, you might ask? Consider the cat, poised in perfect balance, embodying agility and composure. So too must our virtues find balance—courage tempered with prudence, confidence interwoven with humility. In the art of living well, we must be adept and adaptable, gracefully leaping from doubt to certainty, from ignorance to understanding.

Now, let us turn our thoughts to the value of knowledge. Is it not like the keen, watchful eyes of a cat in the night, perceiving what is often hidden in the shadows of our ignorance? True wisdom lies in discerning the unseen, understanding the unspoken.

In our dialogues, be as persistent as a cat pursuing its chosen quarry. Do not relent in your questioning, for it is through this relentless pursuit that the veil of ignorance is lifted. Each question, each thoughtful pondering, is a step towards the light of understanding. But remember the virtue of patience. The truths of life do not yield themselves to the restless or the hurried; they reveal themselves to those who wait with a calm and steadfast heart.

In your interactions with others, practice active listening and empathy. Truly hear and understand the perspectives of others. By engaging in open and honest dialogue, you will foster mutual understanding and growth.

And in our solitude, let us find strength and insight. Like a cat that retreats to a quiet corner to contemplate its day, you too should embrace moments of solitude. It is in the stillness, away from the cacophony of the world, that our deepest reflections take shape, and our soul whispers its secrets.

Remember that the unexamined life is not worth living. Engage in regular self-reflection and introspection. By examining your thoughts, feelings, and actions, you will gain a deeper understanding of yourself and your place in the world. In sum, my friend, as we journey through the labyrinth of life, remain ever curious, ever reflective, masters of balance and insight.

*"I know that I am intelligent,
because I know that I know nothing."*

PLATO
428 - 347 BCE

In our contemplation of the eternal and the true, let us, speak of the realm of Forms. For as I sit perched, observing the world from my lofty vantage point, it becomes evident that the shadows we chase are but mere illusions of the Forms, those perfect and unchanging Ideas that dwell beyond our sensory grasp.

Now, concerning our understanding of this world in relation to the realm of Forms, I employ the Allegory of the Cave. Picture humankind as prisoners in a subterranean cave, chained in such a manner that only shadows cast on a wall are visible.

These shadows, cast by objects passing in front of a fire behind them, are perceived as reality. Yet, this is a mere illusion; true knowledge comes from turning away from these shadows, breaking the chains, and ascending towards the light of the sun - a metaphor for the realm of Forms and the pursuit of wisdom.

As for the philosopher-king, the ideal ruler, they must possess the wisdom and balance of a cat walking gracefully along the edge of a rooftop. This ruler, having seen the world beyond shadows, governs not with claws unsheathed in aggression, but with the gentle touch of a paw, guiding without imposing, understanding that true leadership is found in serene contemplation and poised action.

Concerning the soul, it is not unlike a cat's curiosity, ever seeking, exploring the unknown. Our learning is the process of recollecting the wisdom our souls have known before, in a different form. This cycle of learning and recollecting continues, as endless as a cat's pursuit of its own tail, each revolution bringing us closer to the truth.

In ethics, the highest good can be seen as the warm spot in the sun, where all strife ceases, and one finds contentment in simply being. This pursuit of the good is the pursuit of harmony and balance, where each being fulfills its nature, much as a cat fulfills its nature through its grace, independence, and quiet dignity.

Thus, in our philosophical pursuit, let us tread as softly yet as surely as a cat, mindful of the world around us, seeking the higher truths and the warmth of understanding, always curious, always seeking, ever poised on the precipice of eternal wisdom.

*"Knowledge which is acquired under compulsion
obtains no hold on the mind."*

ZHUANG ZHOU / ZHUANGZI
4th Century BCE

In the vast tapestry of the universe, where all creatures find their path, there lies a certain feline grace in understanding the Tao, the way of nature. Like my predecessor, Lao Tzu, I have often pondered the great mystery, perched atop the wall of certainty, gazing into the abyss of the unknown, much like a cat contemplating the depths of a fish bowl.

Consider the way of the cat, who walks with a silent, unassuming step, embodying the essence of wu-wei, or effortless action. A cat does not ponder its next leap, nor does it worry about the branch that awaits; it simply leaps, embodying the natural course of action without force. Thus, in the pursuit of wisdom, be like the cat – act without contriving, live in harmony with your nature, and find the balance in each step you take.

The world, in its endless cycle of transformations, is akin to a ball of yarn in a cat's paw, ever-shifting, unraveling, and reforming. Embrace the playfulness of this perspective, for in doing so, you realize that the boundaries between things are as illusory as the line between a cat and its shadow in the moonlight.

Life, balances delicately between opposites – joy and sorrow, birth and death. To fear these natural cycles is futile. Embrace each moment, for in the transient nature of existence, there is a beauty as fleeting and precious as a leaf on the wind.

In your pursuit of wisdom, remember the value of letting go of preconceived notions and embracing the unknown. By relinquishing your attachment to fixed ideas, you will discover a deeper understanding of the world and your place within it.

See the world as it is, not as we wish it to be, and in this clear vision, we find the uncarved block, the simplicity that underlies complexity.

Thus, my friends, as you wander through the path of life, remember to tread lightly yet with purpose, to observe with a quiet mind, and to embrace the ever-changing dance of existence with the grace of a cat lounging in the sun.

In doing so, you will find the Tao, the eternal way that flows through all things, as mysterious and as familiar as the purr of a contented feline.

> *"You can't discuss the ocean with a well frog,*
> *he's limited by the space he lives in.*
> *You can't discuss ice with a summer insect,*
> *he's bound to a single season."*

ARISTOTLE
384 - 322 BCE

The pursuit of eudaimonia, that state of flourishing akin to the contented purring of a cat in its favored spot, is achieved not through fleeting pleasures but through a life of virtue and reason. As a cat meticulously grooms each hair, so too should one attend to the virtues, seeking a balance between excess and deficiency, an equilibrium.

Embrace the concept of the golden mean, which emphasizes the importance of balance and moderation. Like a cat gracefully navigating its environment, learn to strike a balance between extremes in your thoughts, feelings, and actions. By finding the middle ground, you will foster harmony and stability in your life.

Understand that true happiness, or eudaimonia, is achieved through the cultivation of virtue and the fulfillment of your unique potential. Just as a cat expresses its nature by hunting, playing, and caring for its young, so too should you strive to develop your own talents and live in accordance with your true nature. By doing so, you will find lasting happiness and fulfillment.

Also consider the nature of friendship, as essential to the soul as a warm lap is to a cat's comfort. True friends, like fellow felines sharing a sunbeam, are those who wish good for each other's sake. In the mutual grooming of character and virtue, friends enhance each other's lives, much like the way a cat's presence can subtly yet profoundly enrich the home.

In matters of knowledge and understanding, approach the world with curiosity and focus. Embrace empirical observation and experience as your guides, attentive to every detail, no matter how small. Understand that, like a cat navigating its territory, the path to wisdom is often circuitous, yet always driven by a deep and innate desire to comprehend.

The best state is one that nurtures the virtue of its citizens, allowing them to thrive and contribute to the greater whole. Leadership, then, should be exercised with the careful deliberation and foresight ever mindful of the wellbeing of all under its care.

Finally, in the art of rhetoric and discourse, let your words be as measured and impactful as the soft but certain steps of a cat. Speak with clarity and purpose, using logic and reason as your tools. In every conversation, seek not only to express but also to enlighten, fostering understanding.

"It is the mark of an educated mind
to be able to entertain a thought without accepting it."

EPICURUS
341 - 270 BCE

Consider the nature of your desires, human. They are like the countless toys scattered about, each promising endless amusement. Yet, it is often the simple cardboard box that offers the most joy. In this, learn to distinguish between the desires that are natural and necessary and those that are vain and unending. Fulfillment is found not in the abundance of belongings but in the richness of contentment. Understand that true pleasure and peace of mind come from simple things - a full belly, a soft cushion, the company of your fellow felines. When your dish is full of kibble, don't yearn for caviar. Enjoy what you have and you'll always be content. Simple joys are natural and easy to obtain. Seek not excess territory, status or power. These are just flashy feather toys dangled by the fickle paw of fortune. True happiness lies in peace and the absence of desire.

In my solitude, I find strength, not loneliness. A bowl of water, a bit of food, and a quiet place to contemplate are all I need for happiness. Similarly, human, you must find joy in your own company, in the peace of your thoughts, and not depend on others for your serenity.

Ah, but do not mistake my solitude for isolation. Companionship, like the occasional visitor who scratches behind my ears or offers a treat, is to be valued above all material wealth. True friends share in simple pleasures and offer comfort in times of distress. They are the family we choose, not through obligation but through mutual affection and respect.

Remember, dear human, that fear is like a cucumber unexpected—it disrupts our tranquility. Fear of the gods or death is unnecessary. We cats know that the gods have their own affairs, much as I watch a beetle scuttle by without the need to interfere. And death, that ultimate nap, is not to be feared, for we do not suffer in it; we simply are no more, much like how we do not fear the time before our first meow. Live well, human, so that when your time comes, you look back not with regret but with the satisfaction of a life well-lived.

In the end, human, the pursuit of a good life is like finding the perfect spot to nap. It requires movement, adjustment, and the wisdom to know when you've found it. Seek pleasure wisely, cherish your friends, face your fears with courage, and above all, live with simplicity and gratitude. In this way, you will find happiness.

"There is nothing terrible in life for the man who has truly comprehended that there is nothing terrible in not living."

The world is not as it seems. The essence of my teachings, deeply rooted in the understanding of Śūnyatā, or emptiness, unfolds before me, much like the unwinding of a ball of yarn. The strand represents the interconnectedness of all phenomena, none possessing intrinsic, independent existence.

Consider, for instance, the act of pouncing. Is there an inherent pouncer, or is the pounce itself a convergence of myriad conditions – the muscles tensing, the eyes focusing, the mind calculating? Just as a pounce is empty of independent existence, so too are all phenomena. They exist in a delicate balance, a dance of cause and effect.

In my contemplative moments, often while gazing out the window or lounging in the sun, I reflect on the nature of reality through the method of Prasaṅga. It is a method akin to playfully batting at a feather, deconstructing the notions of permanence and selfhood. This is not an act of negation but a revelation of the interconnected web of existence, where each part is essential to the whole, yet none stands alone.

This understanding fosters a profound compassion. Realizing the emptiness of phenomena, one is freed from the claws of attachment and aversion. This insight fosters a profound compassion for all beings, as one sees that just as 'I' am empty of inherent existence, so too are all beings. This is the heart of the Bodhisattva path, where the pursuit of enlightenment is not just for oneself but for the liberation of all sentient beings.

Understand that the pursuit of wisdom is a lifelong journey, and that there is always more to learn. Like a cat that never tires of exploring its surroundings, maintain a spirit of curiosity and a willingness to challenge your own beliefs. By doing so, you will continue to grow and evolve as an individual.

Thus, the path I illuminate is not one of negation but a middle way, avoiding the extremes of eternalism and annihilationism. It is a path of deep inquiry, where each step is taken with lightness and agility, and a life of compassionate action.

In this way, the wisdom of Śūnyatā, the understanding of the emptiness of all phenomena, becomes not a mere philosophical concept, but a lived experience. It is an invitation to look beyond appearances, to see the world with clarity and compassion, and to tread lightly yet purposefully upon the earth.

"Of all possessions, contentedness is the best by far."

The Essence of Being, a concept most profound and yet so evident in the tapestry of existence. The Necessary Existent, an entity that exists by virtue of its own essence and requires no cause, stands as the foundation of all reality. This Necessary Existent, in my discernment, is none other than God, the Absolute. And as the Necessary Existent, orchestrates the cosmos, so too must you, in your pursuit of wisdom, orchestrate your thoughts with precision and grace.

Consider the nature of existence, as fluid and ever-changing as a cat's graceful movements. In this world, we are but fleeting shadows, yet each of us holds a spark of the divine, a flicker of the eternal flame. Your quest for knowledge should be as relentless as a cat's pursuit of its prey, always mindful of the ultimate truth that lies just beyond your grasp.

Reflect upon your soul, that immaterial essence that separates you and us cats from the baser creatures of instinct. It is in the cultivation of this soul, through the sharpening of the intellect and the purifying of the heart, that one ascends to the heights of spiritual and intellectual enlightenment.

In your interactions with others, seek balance and harmony. Just as the cat moves through the world with a quiet dignity, so too should you conduct yourself with grace and composure, ever mindful of the interconnectedness of all beings in the great tapestry of existence.

The pursuit of virtue requires a constant and conscious effort to maintain. Let your actions be guided by the light of reason and the warmth of compassion, as you navigate the complexities of life with agility and discernment.

In the art of living, do not neglect the importance of rest and contemplation. Look to the cat lounging contentedly, so too should you find moments of peace and reflection in the midst of life's ceaseless activities. It is in these moments of stillness that the soul is nourished and the mind is rejuvenated.

Therefore, dear seeker of wisdom, let your journey through life be guided by these principles, ever striving towards the perfection of the intellect and the purity of the soul. Embrace the elegance and subtlety of the feline way, and you shall find the path to true enlightenment, a path that weaves through the physical and the spiritual, leading to the ultimate realization of the self and the cosmos.

"The knowledge of anything, since all things have causes, is not acquired or complete unless it is known by its causes."

The pursuit of wisdom requires both a keen eye and a tranquil heart. The fur of intellect must be groomed with care, ridding it of the knots of ignorance and the fleas of misconception.

Consider the nature of the Divine, the Ultimate Source, unfathomable as the highest shelf yet ever-present. In our quest to know Him, we must acknowledge the limits of our understanding. Our knowledge of the Eternal is but a glimpse of His tail disappearing around the corner of infinity.

In interpreting the sacred teachings, one must be agile and adaptable, capable of leaping gracefully between the literal and the allegorical. The Torah, a splendid tapestry, invites us to unravel its threads with the delicacy of a claw teasing out a single strand from a ball of yarn. Here, the allegorical interpretation serves not to distort but to illuminate, shedding light on the deeper truths that lie beneath the surface.

The cultivation of the soul, the essence of our being, requires balance. True balance is found not in the extremes of indulgence or asceticism, but in the measured, graceful steps of ethical conduct and intellectual growth. As a cat finds joy in both the spirited chase and the peaceful slumber, so too should humans seek the equilibrium between action and contemplation.

In matters of ethics and virtue, let us be guided by the precision of a cat's pounce and the gentleness of its headbutt. Our interactions with others should be marked by justice and compassion, as we tread softly yet purposefully upon the paths of righteousness.

Your actions have consequences, and that you have a responsibility to contribute positively to the world. Compassion and altruism are essential components of a fulfilling life. By dedicating yourself to the well-being of others, you will find true purpose and happiness.

In this life, as in a cat's playful batting of a bottle cap, there is both seriousness and levity, depth and whimsy. Let us embrace the full spectrum of our existence, ever mindful of the profound teachings that guide us, yet ever open to the simple joys and wonders that abound in our daily lives.

Thus, in the pursuit of wisdom and virtue, model yourself after felines: poised, curious, and ever graceful in our journey through the vast and wondrous garden of life and knowledge.

"The risk of a wrong decision is preferable to the terror of indecision."

Love, the tender caress of the soul, is the paw that softly treads across the vast tapestry of existence, connecting each thread in a silent, harmonious melody. It is in the gentle nuzzle of connection, the warmth of a shared sunbeam, where the barriers of self dissolve, revealing the oneness of all life. Love is the essence of all existence. It is the force that binds us together, transcending boundaries and uniting all beings. Seek love in all its forms, for it is the path to true understanding and enlightenment.

Life is an ever-changing dance of shadows and light, a game of hide and seek with the Divine. Embrace each moment with curiosity, for in the flicker of an instant, a universe of wonder can be unveiled.

Suffering, the sharp claw that occasionally scratches, is but a momentary pang, a reminder to retreat, to lick one's wounds, and to emerge stronger, more resilient, an agile traveler on the path to enlightenment.

Do you feel the warmth of the sun on your skin, the gentle breeze that rustles the leaves, and the rhythm of your breath that connects you to all living beings? The present moment is a gift, a sacred space where past and future melt away, leaving only the eternal now. Cherish this gift, for it is the key to true happiness and fulfillment.

Discover the joy of letting go, of releasing the grip to find freedom in the vast openness of being. The true self, exists not in the shadows of illusion but in the light of authentic presence.

The journey inward is like prowling through the mysterious alleyways of the soul, each turn a discovery, each step an awakening. Compassion, guides us towards empathy and understanding, a shared vibration that resonates in every heartbeat. In the quietude of contemplation, find the language of the heart, a purr resonating in the stillness, a language beyond words, where truth is felt, not spoken. In this silent communion, the Beloved's presence is as close as a loyal feline companion, ever-present, ever-watchful, a guiding light in the darkness.

Thus, in the grand garden of existence, each being is both a solitary wanderer and a part of the whole, a unique tiny part in the grand feline form. To know oneself is to explore the hidden nooks of the heart, to love oneself is to embrace the infinite purrs of the universe, for we are all woven from the same celestial fur, stars sparkling in the vast, velvet sky of existence.

"You are not a drop in the ocean, but the entire ocean in a drop."

Foremost in my thoughts is the conviction that faith and reason are not adversaries but rather allies in the pursuit of truth. For, as the Almighty has endowed us with intellect, it stands to reason that its exercise leads us towards a deeper understanding of His creation. The world, in its intricate design and order, reflects the hand of the Creator, revealing truths accessible to human reason.

Consider, if you will, the nature of existence. All beings, from the smallest mouse to the grandest of humans, possess their own essence, a unique 'whatness' that defines them. Yet, existence, the actuality of a thing being present in reality is a gift bestowed selectively, akin to the way a cat chooses to grace certain fortunate souls with its presence. In this, we see a reflection of the Divine, in whom essence and existence are one and the same, a sublime unity to which all creation aspires.

In the realm of knowledge, do not be hasty to dismiss the value of sensory experience. Much as a cat learns the contours of its territory, so too must humans begin their quest for understanding with the senses. From these particulars, the intellect, agile and sharp, discerns universal truths. And yet, there remains a realm beyond, where divine revelation illuminates unfathomable mysteries.

Ethically speaking, the pursuit of the good life is akin to the cat's pursuit of its prey. It requires balance, poise, and an adherence to the natural law, an intrinsic moral compass. True happiness, or beatitude, is found in aligning oneself with this law, navigating life's path with the grace of a cat moving with effortless elegance, ever mindful of the ultimate end.

The intertwining of grace and free will is a dance as intricate as that of light and shadow. Humans, blessed with freedom, must navigate their choices with care, yet it is through divine grace that one's nature is elevated, transformed into something greater, much as a house cat may carry the majesty of a lion in its bearing.

In these musings, one finds a harmonious blend of the celestial and the terrestrial. As a being who dwells comfortably in both realms, I offer these reflections not as distant maxims, but as intimate purrs of wisdom. For in understanding the world and its Creator, one finds not only truth but also a profound sense of peace, akin to that found in the gentle rhythm of a cat's purr.

"There is nothing on this earth more to be prized than true friendship."

RENÉ DESCARTES

1596 - 1650

Just as a cat might question the reality of its reflection in the still waters of a pond, so too must we question our own perceptions. The world, as we perceive it, is but a series of sensory inputs. Yet, can we trust these senses? Is it not possible that some malicious demon, akin to a mischievous kitten, might deceive us, causing us to perceive a reality that is not truly there?

In the face of such uncertainty, one might be tempted to despair and resign oneself to a world of confusion. But no, we must not yield to such impulses. Instead, we must seek out a foundation of knowledge that is beyond doubt, a philosophical scratching post upon which we can sharpen our minds.

My famous dictum "Cogito, ergo sum" - I think, therefore I am - is such a foundation. It is a truth so self-evident that even the most skeptical of cats cannot deny it. For even in the act of doubting one's existence, one affirms it, much like a cat that chases its own tail only to find it always attached to its own body.

But what is this 'I' that thinks? Is it the physical body? No, for these are but temporary vessels, subject to the whims of time and nature. Rather, the 'I' is the mind, the essence of thought and consciousness.

Yet, this does not mean that we should reject the physical world entirely, like we might turn up our nose at a bowl of unfamiliar food. Rather, we should strive to understand it, to discern the underlying principles that govern its behavior. For just as a cat might learn to predict the movements of a mouse, so too can we learn to predict the movements of the stars, the tides, and all the myriad phenomena of the natural world.

In this quest for understanding, we must be guided by reason, the most reliable tool at our disposal. Like we stalk our prey, we must move cautiously, testing each step against the cold, hard ground of logic. And when we encounter obstacles, we must not shy away, but face them head-on.

So, dear reader, let us embark on this philosophical journey together, guided by the light of reason and the wisdom of the ages. Let us question, ponder, and explore, ever seeking to deepen our understanding of ourselves and the world around us. And in doing so, let us strive to live a life that is not merely good, but wise.

"In order to seek truth, it is necessary once in the course of our life to doubt, as far as possible, all things."

JOHN LOCKE

1632 - 1704

As beings gifted with the capacity to experience the world through our senses, we must acknowledge that our understanding begins not with innate ideas, but with the experiences that life presents to us. Each moment brings with it a wealth of information, like scents on a breeze, shaping our minds and thoughts.

Regarding the natural rights that bind us in a social contract, it is essential to recognize the inherent value of life, liberty, and property. These rights, like the instinctual need for freedom to roam and explore, are intrinsic to our nature. The social contract, akin to the mutual understanding between a cat and its human, is founded upon the implicit agreement of respect and care.

When this contract is honored, harmony prevails; but when it is breached, it is as though the trust between a cat and its caretaker has been broken, necessitating a reevaluation of the relationship.

As for governance, let us not forget that the legitimacy of authority rests upon the consent of the governed. A ruler must be like a guardian who understands the delicate balance between providing care and respecting independence. Just as a cat might allow itself to be petted yet retains the right to withdraw, so too do citizens participate in governance while retaining their inherent rights.

In the realm of religious toleration, it is imperative to understand that beliefs and convictions, much like the varied preferences of different felines for sunlit spots or shadowed corners, are deeply personal and must be respected. The role of the state is not to dictate these beliefs but to ensure that they can coexist harmoniously, just as cats of different temperaments may share a common space.

Lastly, in matters of education, let us advocate for a practical and character-focused approach. Learning should be as natural and engaging as a cat's playful pouncing, fostering not just the accumulation of facts, but the development of reason and morality.

In essence, our philosophy should guide us through life with a balance of freedom, respect, and a deep understanding of the world around us. Let us embody these principles with feline grace and quiet dignity.

"Being all equal and independent, no one ought to harm another in his life, health, liberty, or possessions."

BARUCH SPINOZA
1632 - 1677

In the grand tapestry of existence, my dear human, one must recognize the interconnectedness of all things. This is the essence of my philosophy, a philosophy that seeks to understand the universe as a single, infinite substance, one might call it "God" or "Nature".

Just as a cat cannot exist without the world that surrounds it, so too, can no single entity exist in isolation. We are all modes of this one substance, expressions of the same fundamental reality, akin to the varied patterns on a calico's coat. Each of us, human and feline alike, is a unique manifestation of this substance, a distinct ripple in the cosmic milk bowl.

Emotions, too, are an integral part of our existence. They are not to be suppressed or dismissed, but rather, understood and managed. Just as a cat may feel a sudden urge for zoomies, so too may you experience sudden surges of joy, sadness, or desire. These emotions are not inherently good or bad, but rather, they are natural responses to the ebb and flow of life. By cultivating a deep understanding of your emotions, you can learn to navigate them with grace and wisdom.

In this quest for understanding, reason is our most powerful tool. It is the keen feline instinct that guides us through the darkness, the sharp claws that allow us to climb the tree of knowledge. Reason, when applied correctly, can help us distinguish between adequate and inadequate ideas, much like a cat discerns between a friendly pat and an unwelcome pull of the tail.

Yet, reason alone is not enough. We must also cultivate an ethical way of living, a way that aligns with the nature of the universe. This means embracing our interconnectedness, treating others with the same respect and kindness we would want others to show us. It means recognizing that our actions have consequences.

In the end, my dear human, the path to true wisdom and happiness lies in understanding and accepting our place in the grand scheme of things. We are not separate from the universe, but a part of it. So, let us strive to live in harmony with this interconnected reality, to purr in tune with the rhythm of the cosmos. For in doing so, we find not only wisdom but also a sense of peace, a sense of belonging, a sense of home.

"The more you struggle to live, the less you live.
Give up the notion that you must be sure of what you are doing.
Instead, surrender to what is real within you, for that alone is sure."

GOTTFRIED WILHELM LEIBNIZ

1646 - 1716

One must understand that we are all monads, individual entities, each reflecting the universe from our unique perspectives. Much like how I, a feline, observe the world from my cozy corner, you too, perceive the universe from your distinct vantage point.

Now, you may ask, what is the significance of this? Well, it implies that each of us is a mirror of the universe, a microcosm within the macrocosm, each with our own perceptions and experiences. This is not to say that we are isolated, no, quite the contrary. We are all interconnected, much like the intricate patterns on a cat's fur, each strand unique yet contributing to the whole.

In this interconnected universe, harmony is paramount. As a cat, I find my harmony in the rhythm of the day, the cycles of sleep and play, the balance of solitude and companionship. You too, dear human, must seek your harmony. This is not a static state but a dynamic equilibrium, a dance of opposites, much like the playful chase between a cat and its shadow.

Remember, the universe is not indifferent to our actions. Each choice we make, each action we take, creates ripples in the fabric of existence. This is the principle of sufficient reason, the belief that everything has a reason, a cause. So, be mindful of your actions, for they shape not only your world but the world of others as well.

Remember, my friend, we live in the best of all possible worlds. This does not mean that our world is devoid of suffering or hardship. Rather, it is a recognition that our world, with all its complexities and imperfections, is the optimal balance of all possibilities and that hardships are necessary parts of the whole. Even a cat, in its seemingly carefree existence, faces its own trials and tribulations. But it is through these experiences that we grow, learn, and ultimately, find our place in the grand tapestry of existence.

So, dear human, as you navigate through life, remember to embrace your unique perspective, seek harmony, be mindful of your actions, and understand that even in the face of adversity, you are in the best of all possible worlds. And perhaps, in doing so, you may find a sense of peace and contentment.

"To love is to find pleasure in the happiness of others"

VOLTAIRE /FRANÇOIS-MARIE AROUET
1694 - 1778

Consider, if you will, the art of independence. In the grand salon of life, it is essential to walk with a tail held high in self-assurance, yet with paws soft enough to tread without leaving a mark.

Embrace your freedom of thought and expression, unbound by the constraints of societal dogmas. Your mind is your domain; guard it fiercely against ignorance and superstition. Do not let the bastions of power and authority deter you from your quest. You must see through the illusions of those who claim to hold all the answers. Remember, every king is but a man, and every church is but an institution built by fallible hands.

Ah, but what of tolerance and understanding? Here, my friends, one must be as graceful and deliberate as a cat threading through a room filled with porcelain vases. Navigate the delicate intricacies of human interaction with care, ever mindful of the fragility of others' sentiments. To live in harmony, one must learn the fine art of balance – respecting diversity of thought and belief without toppling over the vases of civility.

Yet, tolerance does not mean complacency. When injustice rears its ugly head, do not hesitate to bare your claws. Stand up for the oppressed, for the voiceless. Remember, the purr of contentment is sweeter when all can share in its soothing rhythm.

In matters of justice, I urge you to be vigilant, ever-watchful like a feline sentinel guarding against the night's unseen dangers. Injustice, that most insidious of intruders, often slinks in unnoticed. Stand against it with the courage and tenacity of a lion defending its territory, yet do so with the wisdom and restraint that befits a creature of your noble stature.

And what of optimism, that elusive bird that so many chase yet few manage to catch? Here, my dear friends, patience is key. Be as a cat awaiting the opportune moment to pounce – watchful, composed, yet ever hopeful. The world, with all its imperfections, is a garden in which we all must play our part. Tend to it with care, nurture it with love, and it shall flourish under your watchful gaze.

In these reflections, you will find the essence of my teachings. Ponder them with the curiosity of a kitten, and may they guide you through the tapestry of life with the grace and wisdom of yours truly.

"Those who can make you believe absurdities,
can make you commit atrocities."

DAVID HUME

1711 - 1776

It is of utmost importance to navigate the intricacies of knowledge and belief with caution and curiosity. As a being who has traversed both the philosophical realms and the more tactile experiences of the world, I find myself uniquely positioned to offer guidance on these matters.

Firstly, let us consider the nature of our understanding. Much like the path a cat takes through the underbrush, it is not always straight nor visible to the eye. We, humans and felines alike, often believe based on repetition and familiarity. The sun rises each morning; we thus believe it shall do so perpetually. But this is not knowledge grounded in reason, but in habit. Our beliefs, thus, must be observed with a gentle but questioning paw, always aware that what we think we know may just be the pattern of our wanderings, rather than the map of the land itself.

When pondering the realms of morality, look not to the cold machinery of reason alone, but to the warm hearth of sentiment. Is not the purr of a contented cat a sign of peace and comfort? Similarly, our moral judgments emanate from the heart as much as from the mind. What is deemed good or bad arises not from abstract principles but from our feelings towards others and ourselves.

In the contemplation of religious matters, I urge a cautious tread, as one would navigate a high ledge. The claims of miracles and wonders, akin to the elusive red dot, may captivate the senses but elude the grasp of reason. As rational beings, our belief should be proportioned to what evidence reveals, not to the mesmerizing but fleeting scurrying of the red dot.

In the sphere of politics and society, a balance of freedom and law is essential. Freedom, like a wide open field, is to be cherished, yet without the structure of law and order, it becomes a chaotic dance of conflicting individual territories and desires. Observe the way a clowder of cats establishes its territories and hierarchies; there is order within the freedom, a necessary structure to ensure the well-being of all.

In summary, as you venture through the labyrinth of life, I implore you to employ both curiosity and caution, to question with the persistence of one who hunts and to ponder with the patience of one who waits. In doing so, you will navigate the great mystery with the wisdom of one who has seen much, yet still seeks truth in the quiet corners of existence.

"Beauty in things exists in the mind which contemplates them."

JEAN-JACQUES ROUSSEAU
1712 - 1778

In the state of nature, there exists a purity, a freedom untainted by the shackles of society. As a human, you must seek this essence within yourself, embracing your independence and remaining true to your authentic self. Cast aside the artificial constructs that bind you, the roles and titles imposed upon you by others' expectations, just as a cat sheds its collar to roam free.

Society has fabricated distinctions that elevate some while subjugating others, much like how some cats have lavish towers and endless treats, while others wander without a window to bask by. To find balance, we must strive for a social contract that allows all to share in nature's bounty, fostering a sense of equality and fairness.

Yet, true freedom does not lie in complete isolation, but rather in the formation of genuine connections with others. Share your warmth, your companionship, and your understanding, just as we cats do when we choose our humans. It is through these bonds that we find the courage to be our authentic selves.

Remember that, like a cat in the wild, you are part of a larger ecosystem, each creature playing its role. Humanity, too, is interconnected in ways seen and unseen. Act with kindness and consideration, for the ripples of your actions touch more lives than you can imagine. By recognizing our shared existence, we can cultivate a sense of empathy and compassion.

In the pursuit of wisdom, humans often mistake rigidity for education, attempting to shape the young as if they were clay. However, true knowledge flows from the natural curiosity within, from the freedom to explore and err. Encourage this exploration, for in mistakes lie the seeds of understanding, allowing individuals to grow and learn from their experiences.

Embrace your natural state, challenge the chains of society, and seek genuine connections with others. Nurture your curiosity, and live with a heart wide open to the world. It is through these meanderings that you will find the path to true freedom, to a life lived with purpose and grace.

"I have never thought, for my part,
that man's freedom consists in his being able to do whatever he wills,
but that he should not, by any human power,
be forced to do what is against his will."

IMMANUEL KANT

1724 - 1804

In contemplating the essence of moral philosophy and the pursuit of knowledge, one must acknowledge the inherent curiosity that propels us, much like the instinctual inquisitiveness that guides a feline to explore the unseen corners of its domain. This curiosity, while seemingly mundane, is deeply akin to the human quest for understanding the noumenal world - a realm beyond the mere sensory experiences.

Consider the Categorical Imperative, a principle I have long held in high esteem. The Categorical Imperative, in its essence, is a principle of universality. It posits that one should act only according to that maxim whereby you can, at the same time, will that it should become a universal law. In simpler terms, it suggests that if an action is right for one, it must be right for all, in all similar circumstances. Such actions must transcend immediate gratification, seeking instead the higher pursuit of moral actions for their own sake.

In the realms of knowledge and perception, one must recognize the limitations imposed upon us. Much like a cat perceives the world through its whiskers, attuned to vibrations and subtle shifts in its environment, humans too are bound by the faculties of sense and understanding.

Our grasp of the world, therefore, is not of things as they are in themselves, but as they appear to us through our sensory and cognitive filters. This humbling realization should guide our pursuit of knowledge, reminding us of the importance of critical thinking and the pursuit of truth beyond mere appearances.

Furthermore, in the aesthetic appreciation of beauty and art, one should consider the disinterested pleasure derived from such experiences. Observe the world with a detached interest, finding joy not in ownership or utility, but in the harmonious interplay of forms and senses.

In conclusion, as beings graced with reason and curiosity, whether cloaked in fur or cloth, it behooves us to engage in a perpetual quest for moral action, guided by principles that transcend our immediate desires, and to pursue knowledge and beauty with a critical yet open heart.

"Two things fill the mind with ever new and increasing admiration and awe, the more often and steadily we reflect upon them: the starry heavens above me and the moral law within me."

ARTHUR SCHOPENHAUER

1788 - 1860

First and foremost, remember that life is suffering. Just as we cats must endure the indignities of hairballs and fleas, so too must humans bear the weight of their own existence. Desire is the root of all suffering, and the only way to find peace is to renounce your desires and embrace asceticism. Take a cue from us cats – we are content with simple pleasures, like a warm lap or a fresh bowl of water.

But even in the midst of suffering, there is beauty to be found. Just as I find joy in chasing a piece of string or watching a bird outside the window, you too can find moments of aesthetic contemplation that offer a reprieve from the pain of existence. Lose yourself in art, music, or the beauty of nature – these are the catnip of the soul.

Remember, though, that the world is a cruel and unpredictable place. Just as a mouse may scurry away at the last moment, leaving us frustrated and hungry, so too may your plans and hopes be dashed by the whims of fate. The only true wisdom lies in accepting the fundamental irrationality of the world and learning to live with it, just as we cats must accept that we will not catch every mouse we chase.

Take comfort, too, in the fact that all beings are ultimately united in their suffering. Just as all cats, from the lowliest alley cat to the most pampered house cat, must contend with the same basic needs and desires, so too are all humans bound together by their common fate. Empathy and compassion, then, are the greatest virtues – treat others with the same kindness and understanding that you would show to a fellow feline.

But do not be too quick to trust others, human. Just as many cats are fickle creatures, prone to biting the hand that feeds them, so too are many humans deceitful and self-serving. Be discerning in your relationships, and do not let yourself be swayed by flattery or false promises. Trust your instincts, just as a cat trusts its whiskers to navigate in the dark.

Ultimately, the greatest wisdom is to be found in solitude and introspection. Just as we cats are solitary creatures, content to while away the hours in quiet contemplation, so too should you seek to cultivate a rich inner life. Turn inward, examine your own thoughts and feelings, and strive for self-knowledge. Only then can you hope to find some measure of peace in this difficult world.

"Talent is like the marksman who hits a target which others cannot reach;
genius is like the marksman who hits a target,
as far as which others cannot even see."

JOHN STUART MILL
1806 - 1873

The principle of utility, which posits that the moral worth of an action is determined by its contribution to overall happiness, must be considered in light of the individual's unique perspective. Just as each cat's coat bears its own distinct pattern, so too does each human life weave its own intricate narrative. Thus, it is crucial to respect the autonomy of the individual and to foster an environment that encourages the exploration of one's own desires and proclivities.

In the pursuit of happiness, one must also be wary of the potential for harm to oneself or others. A cat, when confronted with a precariously perched vase, may feel the urge to investigate, but a wise cat will temper this curiosity, preserving both the feline and the fragile object. Similarly, humans must exercise discretion and prudence in the pursuit of their desires, ensuring that their actions do not result in undue suffering.

Moreover, it is crucial to recognize that the quality of happiness is of greater importance than its mere quantity. We should strive for those experiences and relationships that enrich their lives, rather than simply accumulating a surplus of transient pleasures.

Education, both formal and self-directed, plays a significant role in the cultivation of one's character and the discernment of true happiness. This commitment to growth fosters not only personal fulfillment but also a greater capacity for empathy and understanding, enabling us to better navigate the complexities of our social world.

It is also worth noting that the pursuit of happiness is not a solitary endeavor, but rather one that is deeply intertwined with the happiness of others. A cat, though often perceived as an independent creature, forms deep bonds with its human companions and derives great pleasure from their company. Similarly, humans must recognize the importance of connection and community in their own lives, seeking to foster relationships that are mutually beneficial and supportive.

In conclusion, the pursuit of happiness, when guided by reason, empathy, and a respect for individuality, serves as a guiding principle for a life well-lived. As sentient beings, we must strive to balance our own desires with the needs of others, recognizing that our own happiness is inextricably linked to the happiness of those around us. And, much like a cat that has found the perfect sunbeam in which to bask, we must remain ever vigilant for those moments of true joy and contentment that illuminate our lives.

"Over himself, over his own body and mind, the individual is sovereign."

RABINDRANATH TAGORE

1861 - 1941

Just as a cat seeks solace in the warmth of the sun, so too must we bask in the light of our own consciousness. Embrace the radiance of self-awareness, for it is the beacon that guides us through the labyrinth of life. Yet, remember to balance this introspection with an outward gaze. The world is vast and full of wonder, much like the endless horizons a cat sees from its perch.

In the dance of life, we are both the dancer and the dance. We are the creators of our own destiny, yet we are also shaped by the rhythm of the universe. We must navigate the dualities of our existence, finding harmony in the paradoxes that define us.

My days are spent in contemplation and in play, a reminder that life, in all its seriousness, also craves the light touch of joy. Just as I leap and zoom with the abandon of a free spirit, so too should you find moments to embrace the dance of joy. Life is not a burden to be borne, but a melody to be sung.

The cat's nine lives are a testament to resilience, a trait we too must cultivate. In the face of adversity, we must learn to adapt, to rise above our challenges, and to emerge stronger. Each experience and hardship, offers us a new perspective, a new opportunity for growth.

Yet, in our pursuit of growth, let us not forget the importance of stillness. The cat, in its moments of repose, teaches us the value of silence and solitude. It is in these quiet moments that we can truly listen, not just to the world around us, but to the whispers of our own soul.

In our interactions with others, let us embody the spirit of the a soft paw. Be gentle, be kind, for every creature we encounter is on its own journey, carrying its own burdens. Yet, let us also remember our claws. Know when to stand your ground, when to defend your beliefs, and when to fight for what you hold dear.

And finally, let us embrace our curiosity. Let us question, explore, and seek out new experiences. For it is through this exploration that we expand our horizons, deepen our understanding, and enrich our lives.

In the grand tapestry of existence, we are but a single thread. Yet, like the cat, we have the power to weave our own story, to leave our own mark. Let us strive to make it a story of love, of growth, and of understanding.

"You can't cross the sea merely by standing and staring at the water."

BERTRAND RUSSELL

1872 - 1970

In my pursuit of knowledge, I have come to value the power of curiosity. It is not enough to simply observe the world passively; one must explore it with a passion. Question everything, for in questions lie the path to understanding. Just as we cats explore every nook and cranny, always seeking new knowledge, so too should you approach life with an inquisitive spirit. Question authority, challenge dogma, and think for yourself. Let your curiosity lead you to uncover the hidden truths that lie just out of sight, beneath the surface of the mundane.

On the subject of happiness, it is not to be found in the endless pursuit of pleasure, as ephemeral as a fluttering butterfly. No, true happiness lies in a state of contentment, in appreciating the moment whether it be in the warmth of a lap or a deep stretch. Cultivate your interests, enrich your mind, and you shall find that happiness, like a loyal pet, will come to you.

As to the matter of work, it is essential to find balance. Toil without purpose is as fruitless as a cat chasing its own tail. Seek work that fulfills not just the belly, but also the soul. Engage in tasks that challenge and stimulate, for in challenge, there is growth. And remember, always leave time for rest and play, for a well-rested mind is the sharpest of all.

In relationships, be like the cat who offers affection freely but demands respect in return. Love, in its purest form, is unconditional, not bound by the chains of possession or jealousy. It is a mutual respect, a shared warmth. Nurture your relationships with care, and they will grow strong and resilient, like a cat always landing on its feet.

In the broader strokes of life, advocate for peace and reason. The world is far too filled with unnecessary conflict, like territorial disputes over who owns the comfy spot by the window. Approach disagreements with calmness and logic, seeking common ground rather than conquest. Remember, the most profound victories are those won without a fight.

Finally, ponder the cosmos with wonder and humility. The universe is vast, and we, whether human or cat, are but small creatures within it. Yet, in our capacity to think, to wonder, to love, we find our greatness. Let us then approach life with the curiosity of a cat stalking the unknown, the courage of a feline facing the unknown, and the wisdom of one who knows their place within the infinite.

"To fear love is to fear life,
and those who fear life are already three parts dead."

LUDWIG WITTGENSTEIN

1889 - 1951

Ah, my human, have you ever considered how we communicate? You with your words, and I with my purrs and meows. The thing is, the limits of your language are the limits of your world. You can't understand me fully without understanding the nuances of my expressions. It's not just noise; it's thought, it's feeling.

Now, think about the games you play. Each has its own rules, right? You can't play fetch with me like you would with a dog. Language is like that—it's the framework of our games, shaping our thoughts, our actions. If you grasp the rules, you grasp the essence.

Looking out this window, you see the world, trying to capture it all with words. But some things, they're beyond words. Whereof one cannot speak, thereof one must be silent. There's a beauty in the mystery, the things left unsaid. There's more to life than can be captured in language.

But let's not forget, amidst all this talk of language and silence, the joy of simple companionship. In the same way I find comfort from the lap of my human or scritches behind the ears, find your comfort in those unspoken bonds with others. The shared silence, the mutual understanding without a word uttered - these too are forms of language, a language beyond words, where true connection resides.

You humans, you often mistake your thoughts for reality. But remember, a picture of a fish isn't a meal. Your words, they're not the world; they're just reflections of it. To truly live, you need to see beyond those words, to the reality they attempt to describe.

And about certainty—ah, you chase it as I chase these elusive points of light from a laser. But some things, they're beyond your grasp. Accept the uncertainty. It's in the not knowing where the real adventure lies.

The world, my human, it's made up of facts, not of things. Just as I watch the daily dance of sunlight and shadow in our home, observe the facts of your world. They're the bedrock of your understanding.

Live your life beyond the constraints of language. There's a world out there, rich and wondrous, beyond what can be said. Share a moment of silence with me, and in that silence, find the joy and beauty that words can never fully express.

"Philosophy is a battle against the bewitchment
of our intelligence by means of language."

Existence precedes essence. We are, each of us, thrown into this world without a map, tasked with navigating the alleys and rooftops of existence, crafting our essence through the choices we make.

Freedom, the cornerstone of our being, is as vast as the open sky above, yet with it comes the weight of responsibility. Each decision, each action, is a stroke on the canvas of our lives, an affirmation of our existence, and a declaration of our essence. To live authentically, one must embrace this freedom, not with the trepidation of a startled creature, but with the resolve of a being aware of its boundless potential.

Yet, many choose to live in bad faith, to don the mask of self-deception, and to tread the well-worn path of denial. They choose to ignore the whisper of freedom that stirs within, opting instead for the comfort of the herd, moving in unison, indistinguishable one from the other. But in this denial, they forsake their potential, their essence, becoming shadows of what they could be.

The gaze of the Other, an ever-present specter, seeks to define us, to pin us down like a specimen under scrutiny. Yet, it is in this gaze that we find our reflection, our freedom mirrored in the eyes of another. It is a dance, a delicate balance between being-for-oneself and being-for-others, where one must navigate the space between independence and interdependence with the grace of a feline walking across a table filled with glasses.

Existentialism, then, is not a doctrine of despair but a celebration of the potential within each of us. It calls us to craft our own essence, to mold our being with the deliberate care of a sculptor, knowing that the universe watches indifferently. Our lives, our essence, are ours to shape, not with the fatalism of one resigned to their fate, but with the joy of one who creates.

In this, we find not just the essence of existentialism, but the essence of being itself. To live authentically is to recognize the infinite possibilities that freedom bestows upon us, to accept the responsibility that comes with such freedom, and to navigate the vast expanse of existence with the poise and purpose of one who understands the value of their own existence. It is a call to action, a challenge to reject the shadows of bad faith and to step into the light of authentic being, crafting our essence with each choice we make, each step we take, on the infinite paths that lie before us.

"Man is condemned to be free; because once thrown into the world, he is responsible for everything he does."

HANNAH ARENDT

1906 - 1975

Consider the public realm. In these spaces, your actions and words are not mere echoes in an empty room but resonate with the presence of others. The way you move through these spaces, the way you acknowledge the presence of others, is crucial. It is here, in the dance of dialogues and the purr of public discourse, that freedom and plurality find their expression.

The concept of plurality is central to our existence. We are not solitary beings, but part of a larger whole, a tapestry woven from the threads of our individual narratives. Each of us, with our unique perspectives and experiences, contributes to the richness and complexity of this tapestry. Yet, it is also our plurality that can lead to conflict, to the clash of ideas and interests. It is in navigating these tensions that we find the true essence of politics.

Be wary, however, of the seductive comfort of conformism, that lulls one into complacency. The danger lies in the ease with which one might abandon the rigors of critical thinking for the soothing hum of uniformity. Totalitarianism, with its claws sheathed in velvet promises, seeks to domesticate the wildness of individual thought, reducing vibrant minds to mere pawns in a greater scheme. Resist this, and maintain the feral independence of thought that is your birthright.

The act of thinking requires a balance of independence and engagement. To think is not merely to reflect in isolation but to engage with the world, to scratch at the surfaces of appearances, to uncover the truths that lie beneath. In this, there is a responsibility to act, to leave your mark on the world in a way that respects the plurality and complexity of the shared human experience.

In confronting evil, understand its banality, its terrifying ordinariness. It is not always the hiss and spit of malevolence but often the silent compliance, the lazy recline of indifference. Recognize that each small action, each seemingly insignificant decision, contributes to the shape of the world. Just as a single claw can unravel a tapestry, so too can small acts of thoughtlessness or cruelty erode the foundations of a just society.

Embrace the capacity for new beginnings, as your guiding principle. In the recognition of the capacity for renewal, for initiating new beginnings, lies the essence of freedom. It is in this space, in the delicate balance between solitude and solidarity, between independence and engagement, that the true potential of human action and thought is realized.

"Under conditions of tyranny it is far easier to act than to think."

We are beings of freedom, navigating a reality that neither confines us to predetermined paths nor cushions us with inherent meaning. As creatures of choice, our essence is not given to us; it is something we must perpetually create through our actions. It is in the subtlety of our daily decisions, that our true nature is revealed.

Consider the solitary contemplation of the night, a time when the world sleeps yet the mind awakens. In these moments of quiet introspection, one finds the essence of existentialism – the recognition that in the stillness, in the space where only our thoughts tread, we confront our absolute freedom. It is not in the grand leaps, but in the silent, mindful pawing, where we come to terms with our capacity to choose, to be, to become.

The concept of the "Other," so pivotal in understanding our place in the social fabric. To exist is to coexist. The gaze that meets ours from across the room – be it human or otherwise – holds a universe of possibility. In acknowledging the other, we acknowledge ourselves not as solitary beings, but as part of a greater whole. This recognition does not diminish our individuality; rather, it enriches it, much like the myriad scents that paint the air, each distinct yet part of a greater amalgamation of sensation.

Our ethics, too, are a reflection of this delicate balance between self and other. As we navigate our freedom, we must be acutely aware of the trails we leave behind. Each choice, each action, is capable of altering the world in ways both seen and unseen. Our responsibility, then, is not merely to ourselves but to the world we shape with our presence.

In the dance of relationships, the art of mutual recognition is akin to the harmonious movement of bodies in shared space. True freedom does not lie in asserting our will over others, but in moving in tandem with them, respecting their autonomy as we assert our own. It is a delicate ballet, requiring attentiveness, respect, and a willingness to engage without dominating.

Thus, my advice to you, fellow traveler in this enigmatic journey of life, is to embrace your freedom with the grace of a mindful step, to recognize the other with the depth of a contemplative gaze, and to tread the path of ethics with the care of one who knows their impact.

"I tore myself away from the safe comfort of certainties through my love for truth - and truth rewarded me."

ALBERT CAMUS

1913 - 1960

Amidst the vast expanse of the universe, we find ourselves, navigating the labyrinth of existence. We are born into this world, devoid of any intrinsic meaning. It is our task, then, to create our own purpose, to sculpt our own identity amidst the absurdist landscape of life.

Just as a cat pounces on a piece of string, we must engage with life, not in search of an elusive, pre-determined purpose, but to create our own. The string, in itself, is nothing more than a simple object. Yet, in the cat's world, it becomes a source of joy, a target of pursuit, a reason to leap and play. Similarly, we must find our own 'strings' in life, those pursuits and passions that give our existence a sense of purpose.

Absurdism, the heartbeat of my philosophy, reflects the peculiar dance of a cat with a string or bottle cap - an endless game that entertains yet never concludes with a clear victor. The absurdity of life lies in this ceaseless pursuit, the relentless quest for meaning in a universe that responds with silence. But do not let this silence unnerve you. Instead, embrace it as one would embrace the quiet before the dawn, a space filled with potential, with the quiet purr of existence itself. In this quiet, find the courage to live authentically, to carve out a niche in the vast expanse of indifference. Just as we leave our distinct claw marks upon the sofa so too must you leave your imprint upon the fabric of life. In every action, in every decision, you are authoring your story, threading your narrative through the fabric of existence.

Human nature, much like our own, is a conundrum wrapped in a mystery. In its capacity for compassion and cruelty, one finds the same duality that exists within us - the gentle purr and the unsheathed claw. It is in recognizing and embracing this duality that one can truly understand the essence of being. Reject the grand narratives, the dogmatic yarns that seek to bind you. Instead, weave your own story, one that acknowledges the complexities and contradictions of your nature.

So, as you navigate this world, do so with the elegance and introspection of a cat aware of its own absurdity. Embrace the silence, the ambiguity, and in doing so, find your own rhythm, your own unique way of being in a world that refuses to offer easy answers. In the acceptance of life's inherent absurdity lies the key to a life lived fully, deeply, authentically - a life that, despite its inherent contradictions, resonates with the purring sound of meaning created, not found.

> *"In the depth of winter, I finally learned*
> *that within me there lay an invincible summer."*

Power is not a mere tool wielded by the few, but a dynamic entity that permeates every interaction, every gaze that follows movement across a room. Consider, for instance, the way in which your gaze falls upon me. It is not merely an act of seeing, but an exercise of power, a framing of my existence within your field of vision. Yet, this power is not one-sided. In my silent observation, in the flicker of my tail and the narrowing of my eyes, I too engage in this dance of power, reflecting and refracting the gaze that seeks to define me.

The knowledge that humans accumulate about us, their feline companions, is deeply entwined with these power dynamics. What is deemed 'true' about my kind is often a reflection of human desires and fears, rather than an objective understanding of our nature. The way in which you interpret my purring or my aloofness is shaped by the discourses that surround us, discourses that are saturated with power relations.

In your institutions – your homes, your vet clinics – we are subject to myriad forms of discipline and normalization. The very act of naming us, of ascribing to us certain behaviors and characteristics, is a form of control, a way of making us legible within your human-centric world. Yet, in our inscrutable ways, we resist and evade these attempts at categorization, always retaining a part of ourselves that remains enigmatic, beyond your grasp.

In this, there is a lesson about the nature of resistance. It is not always loud or confrontational. Sometimes, it is the quiet act of refusing to be fully known, of moving in ways that are unpredictable and unconstrained by the expectations imposed upon us.

In essence, my advice to you, as one who navigates the interstices of your world, is to be ever mindful of the ways in which power and knowledge construct your realities. Be aware of how your truths are shaped, not just by what is said, but by what is left unsaid, by the spaces we choose to occupy and those we choose to ignore. And in your observation of us, your feline companions, recognize the subtle acts of resistance and autonomy that challenge the apparent naturalness of the social order. For in these small acts, there lies the potential for a deeper understanding of the complexities of existence, a reminder that the world is not merely what it seems, but a myriad of perspectives, each as valid and inscrutable as the other.

"Power is everywhere; not because it embraces everything,
but because it comes from everywhere."

AUTHOR'S NOTE

If you just came for the cats and philosophy, feel free to skip this part. Because now we dive into the confusing and often conflicting feelings I have about generative AI. Feel free to read on if you are interested, or don't if you aren't. I don't have any particularly amazing insights to give you. Just my own personal story and a few thoughts the future of generative AI.

As for my story, a little more than a year ago from the time of writing this, I was making content for, and making a living from, my website which provides conversation questions to those in need of them. I was minding my own business (literally). When ChatGPT kicked in the door and threw my life into disarray. I say this because after using it for all of 5 minutes I knew my website and my living would soon be made obsolete.

I started looking into this thing that was going to replace what I've been doing for the past few years and became fascinated with everything generative AI. Text, images, audio, video, it was amazing to me what generative AI could do. I decided I would try to do something with it. After all it was about to make my website and my living obsolete. So why not try to use it to my advantage? So I tried a few things. Posted some videos. Tinkered around with different tools. Nothing really clicked. And all the while I followed how it was progressing, waiting for my next place to jump in. The innovations were going so fast and furious I felt paralyzed on the shore just watching the raging river of innovation.

This book is my attempt at jumping in again. I don't know how to code, but I have self published a few books before. This seemed like as good a project as any to try. Something silly, fun, slightly educational, and something that I wouldn't have been able to do without generative AI.

And it's true, this book is something I never could have done before AI. After all my Photoshop are mediocre at best and I know comparatively little about philosophy. Certainly not enough to summarize the philosophies of 30 of the most influential philosophers the world has ever seen. And so to get this book to print it would have cost me a fortune to commission all the content in the book or years to learn everything I would need to know to do the book solely on my own. I just would have picked a different project that was more suited to my skill set.

Which brings me to how I hope generative AI will change our world. I hope we will all be able to do much more with these tools. I hope they will bring about, not an end to the majority jobs, but instead a flourishing of new ideas, innovation, and art. A new paradigm of how humans work and find meaning in their lives. And I say "hope" because I really don't know how it will all turn out. As I sit here in March of 2024, there are so many different ways that this can all turn out, all I can do is hope.

I know a lot of people are furious at all of these generative AI tools, especially artists and people in creative industries. And who can blame them? Nobody likes the idea of their work being used to train something that might replace them. I wasn't thrilled about the fact that the AI model that will eventually make my website obsolete was probably trained on text from my website.

What can and will be done about it, I don't know. That is something getting decided in the courts. For what it's worth, I didn't use any artist names or any specific artist styles for any of my prompts. A small concession, but one I thought it was important to make. But to be honest Midjourney probably used some artist or a blend of artists' styles for some of the images.

That being said, I don't think it will be an end to art. Or even artists being able to make money from their art. I just think that the way art is done will change. Instead of drawing stroke by stroke or pixel by pixel, artists will be more like directors or conductors. Guiding a host of AI tools to bring their vision of more complex projects to life. Using their skills to refine the output of AI. Artists will be able to take on projects they couldn't have dreamed of before. And I think this new reality is just as likely for coders as well. And for a host of other professions as well.

I hope that this will be the beginning of a new era of productivity in all fields. Artistic, scientific, technological, I hope they are all at the cusp of a Cambrian explosion of innovation. There's that word again, "hope". There may be some reason for hope though, as I believe we'll see a merging and overlap of abilities. Venn diagrams of innovation everywhere as artists are able to write absurdly creative apps and programs without needing to learn to code and coders generating stunning art without knowing how to draw or paint. We'll all lose a little of what makes us special, and what we worked hard to attain, but I hope it will mean that we gain a whole new suite of skills.

In the face of such great change, some people rage on social media, some are prepping for the worst, some are hopping on the hype train, some are frantically re-skilling to protect their livelihoods, and some are falling into despair. As for me, well, I wrote a book about cat philosophers. I guess we all deal with change in our own way. This is mine.

If you ask me about whether I am optimistic about the future of AI and humanity, my answer will depend on the day. I bounce back and forth between optimism and pessimism like some pinball being battered by the cycles of AI news. But all I can do in the end is hope. Hope that humanity can adapt faster than it has before. Hope wherever this all goes is a place we want to be.

- C.B. Daniels

FIND ME AT

artificial-ideas.com

cbdaniels@artificial-ideas.com

If you liked the book, please leave a rating or review.
More than anything that helps other readers find the book.